WIND ENERGY

ABDO
Publishing Company

INNOVATIVE TECHNOLOGIES

WIND ENERGY

BY MELISSA HIGGINS

CONTENT CONSULTANT

Erik E. Nordman, PhD

Assistant Professor, Natural Resources Management

Grand Valley State University

CREDITS

Published by ABDO Publishing Company, PO Box 398166, Minneapolis, MN 55439. Copyright © 2013 by Abdo Consulting Group, Inc. International copyrights reserved in all countries. No part of this book may be reproduced in any form without written permission from the publisher. The Essential Library™ is a trademark and logo of ABDO Publishing Company.

Printed in the United States of America,
North Mankato, Minnesota

092012
012013

 THIS BOOK CONTAINS AT LEAST 10% RECYCLED MATERIALS.

Editor: Rebecca Felix
Series Designer: Craig Hinton

Photo Credits: Stephen Meese/Shutterstock Images, cover; Stephan Drescher/iStockphoto, 6; David Sprott/Shutterstock Images, 9; Fotolia, 10, 56, 78; Royal Photographic Society/SSPL/Getty Images, 12; Anthony Potter Collection/Getty Images, 15; Sal Veder/AP Images, 19; Bas Meelker/Shutterstock Images, 21; Shutterstock Images, 22, 64, 74, 80, 82, 101; Dorling Kindersley/DK Images, 25; Red Line Editorial, 26, 30, 36, 37; Bart Everett/Shutterstock Images, 27; Brian Jackson/Fotolia, 32; Michael Westhoff/iStockphoto, 38 (left); Akhararat Wathanasing/iStockphoto, 38 (right); Colin Salmon (c) Dorling Kindersley/DK Images, 39; Howard Sandler/Shutterstock Images, 41; Todd Klassy/Shutterstock Images, 42; Panoramic Images/Getty Images, 45; Jim Veilleux/iStockphoto, 46; Richard Gillard/iStockphoto, 49; Stefan Ouwenbroek/iStockphoto, 50; Bigstock, 53; Carol Heesen/iStockphoto, 59; Michael Bodmann/iStockphoto, 62; B Brown/Shutterstock Images, 67; VassilisPatrinos/Bigstock, 69; Eric Gevaert/Shutterstock Images, 70; Jeff J Mitchell/Getty Images, 87; Andrew F Kazmierski/iStockphoto, 89; Makani Power, 90; Andrea Swenson Dunlap/Makani Power, 93; Robert Nickelsberg/Getty Images, 95

Library of Congress Cataloging-in-Publication Data
Higgins, Melissa, 1953-
 Wind energy / Melissa Higgins.
   p. cm. -- (Innovative technologies)
 Audience: 11-18.
 Includes bibliographical references and index.
 ISBN 978-1-61783-469-1
 1. Wind power--Juvenile literature. 2. Wind turbines--Juvenile literature. 3. Renewable energy sources--Juvenile literature. I. Title.
 TJ820.H54 2013
 333.9'2--dc23
                          2012024013

>> TABLE OF CONTENTS

CHAPTER 1

WIND ENERGY AT A GLANCE

The wind's power is undeniable. It erodes mountains, tears roofs off buildings, and topples trees. On a smaller scale, an ill-timed wind gust can ruin your summer's day by blowing sand into your hot dog or veering your fly ball into an outfielder's mitt.

Wind can also be harnessed for great benefit. Without wind pushing their ships' sails, Christopher Columbus and other explorers would never have crossed the world's oceans. Inhospitable areas of the arid American West were settled with the help of windmills pumping drinking water from underground springs. These are some amazing accomplishments for something you cannot even see. People have been using wind as an energy source for centuries. With modern technology, power from wind can be captured and converted into electricity that runs homes, factories, and communities.

« Wind's power can range from a light breeze to consistent gusts strong enough to shape landscape features.

WHY WIND?

Inventors and researchers explore new ways to capture wind energy because as the world's population grows, so does the demand for energy. With a growing demand, renewable energy sources are important. Renewable energy has a continual source that is not in danger of running out. Wind is considered renewable because it is created naturally.

Although there is an abundance of wind flowing around the world, another energy source, fossil fuels—such as coal, oil, and natural gas—currently contributes more than 70 percent of the world's energy.[1] Although commonly used, fossil fuels come with many negative effects. Fossil fuels are imperfect sources of energy because they will eventually run out, and they cannot be

ALTERNATIVE, GREEN, FOSSIL—WHAT IS THE DIFFERENCE?

There are several types of energy sources, and they are often labeled with terms that compare newer technologies with conventional technologies. What is the difference between these terms?

Alternative is a broad term referring to energy that comes from a source other than traditional fossil fuels. *Renewable* refers to natural energy that replenishes itself. For example, every day the sun shines (solar energy), the wind blows (wind energy), rivers flow (hydroelectric energy), the earth generates heat (geothermal energy), and plants used for energy regrow (biomass energy). *Sustainable* refers to an energy source that is both renewable and efficient.

An energy source is considered *green* if its extraction and use have a minimal negative impact on the environment. For example, a large hydroelectric dam that prevents fish from migrating upstream may be considered renewable and efficient, but it would not be green. *Fossil fuels*—such as coal, petroleum, and natural gas—are resources that formed under the earth's crust millions of years ago from the remains of animals and plants. Once gone, these resources cannot be replenished.

A factory refining oil for energy use clouds the air with pollution.

replaced. Some energy experts estimate that reserves of oil, a major fossil fuel refined from petroleum, will meet global demand only through the middle of this century.

Searching for and capturing fossil fuels can be a destructive process. When energy developers search for oil or excavate mountaintops for coal, they use a lot of energy and resources in the process and environmental damage often results. Once fossil fuels are obtained, burning them for energy emits particles and gases that can alter and be harmful to the environment by contributing to air pollution and global warming.

US oil is most often obtained from foreign countries. Being dependent on another country for energy is expensive and can threaten national security if the foreign government decides to cut its fuel exports. Since an oil shortage crisis that occurred in the 1970s, the United States and many other countries have been looking for ways to wean themselves off foreign oil. This is one reason, in addition to doing less damage to the environment, that finding alternative energy sources is important.

While there is no single technological answer, wind energy is one option for an alternative energy source that could alleviate some major concerns associated with fossil fuel use. Wind energy does have its share of drawbacks, but many of the technological, environmental, and social problems caused by wind turbines are being addressed. Engineers are making wind turbines more efficient, powerful, cost-effective, quiet, and safe. And new innovations—such as turbines that fly in the sky—mean the coming years may bring changes we have not yet imagined. The cutting-edge innovations on the horizon today arise from a long history of people utilizing the power of wind.

《 Wind energy is one option for clean, renewable energy in the future.

CHAPTER 2

THE HISTORY OF WIND ENERGY

People have harnessed the wind's power since ancient times, but it was inventors in the nineteenth century who first turned wind into electricity. Throughout history, wind's transformation into a global energy source has been shaped by economic, political, and social forces.

THE WINDMILL

It is uncertain who first came up with the idea to construct a windmill to perform everyday tasks, but remains of early windmills have been found in ancient Mesopotamia and Persia. These early machines were vertical-axis windmills, which means the blades rotated around a vertical shaft. The Persian windmill, which dates back as far as 700 CE, was likely used to pump water and grind grain. Its blades were constructed of cloth or straw mats.

 European windmill, 1853

In twelfth-century Europe, the windmill underwent a dramatic change. Its axis shifted from vertical to horizontal, where blades rotated around a horizontal shaft that was level with the ground. The mills from northern Europe, called post mills, were wooden structures with blades that were covered with cloth or wooden slats. The post mill operator would manually turn the structure to face the wind.

In the fourteenth century, smock windmills and tower windmills first came into use. They were taller and more efficient than post mills—only the top caps of the structures needed to be rotated to face the wind. These windmills were used to pump water, reduce wood pulp to paper, power sawmills, grind grain and spices, and pulverize paint pigments, cocoa, and chalk.

WINDMILLS IN THE UNITED STATES

Because they had an abundance of rivers and streams, American colonists built more waterwheels than windmills in the seventeenth and eighteenth centuries. It wasn't until people began settling in the water-poor, wind-rich West in the nineteenth century that windmills truly gained a foothold in North America.

What became known as the American windmill looked very different from its European counterpart. While it had the same horizontal-axis style, the American windmill was smaller and lighter and had more blades than the European versions. By the late nineteenth century, it is

Windmill on a rural farm in Nebraska in the 1930s

estimated that as many as 6 million windmills dotted the US landscape from the Great Plains to the West Coast.[1] While most of these mills pumped water for homes, cattle troughs, and steam-powered locomotives, some were set up to saw wood, churn butter, and raise sand from mines.

ELECTRICITY FROM THE WIND

By the late nineteenth and early twentieth centuries, coal and petroleum were used to generate electricity to power homes and factories. Even though these resources were abundant and a generally inexpensive way to create electricity, it was hard to ignore the free energy source of wind. The first person known to build an electricity-generating wind turbine was Scottish inventor James Blyth in 1887.

The first person to use a wind turbine for large-scale electricity generation was Charles Brush, a wealthy inventor and scientist living in Cleveland, Ohio. Between 1887 and 1888, Brush constructed an 80,000-pound (36,000 kg) windmill in his garden that was 60 feet (18 m) tall. The wind-fed generator supplied 12 kilowatts of power, which fed into approximately 400 batteries located in his mansion. Brush used his windmill through the 1890s to power 350 incandescent lights and several electric motors.

During the late nineteenth century, US cities were becoming electrified, drawing power from centralized utility grids. Rural ranches and farms often were not on the grid, however, because it was expensive for power companies to string the electric lines to them. By the 1920s, several US companies sold electricity-generating windmills, often called wind chargers, to rural dwellers in need of electricity. Hundreds of thousands of wind chargers operated during the

1930s and 1940s. But by the mid-1950s, the Rural Electrification Administration—created in 1935 by President Franklin D. Roosevelt's New Deal administration—had provided most of the rural United States with centralized grids. Centralized, government-subsidized electricity spelled the end of homegrown wind power, and most wind-charger companies went out of business.

FROM ENERGY CRISIS TO AN INDUSTRY

By 1973, the United States and other industrialized nations were heavily dependent on energy from oil, some of which came from Arab countries. A decades-long Arab-Israeli conflict was heating up. Seeking to influence Middle Eastern politics, the Organization of Petroleum Exporting Countries announced it would stop providing oil to any country that sided with Israel in the Arab-Israeli conflict. It also raised the price of its petroleum. Within a few months, the price of oil worldwide quadrupled.[2] The United

ELECTRIFYING RURAL AMERICA

Franklin D. Roosevelt was elected president of the United States in 1932, during the worldwide economic slump known as the Great Depression. As he promised during his campaign, Roosevelt set up a New Deal aiming to bring new prosperity to the country and repair economic damage from recent years. During his first few months as president, Roosevelt passed several bills to reduce poverty and unemployment. He also created the Rural Electrification Administration as part of the New Deal, which would provide electric power to rural areas at reasonable rates to increase labor productivity and improve the quality of life for rural citizens.

States and other oil-importing countries panicked. In the United States, high oil prices led to long lines at gas stations and an economic recession. The US public and most politicians agreed something had to be done about the country's dependence on foreign oil. One solution was developing new and renewable energy, such as wind power.

Due to a combination of tax credits, guaranteed market prices, and areas with ample wind, California became the most popular place in the United States for wind power during the 1980s, representing approximately 90 percent of the world's wind turbines.[3] But by 1985, the federal tax credit expired, oil became affordable again, and many of the wind industry's first attempts at turbines proved fragile or failed. Many investors had left the fledgling wind-energy industry by the late 1980s.

Unlike the US government, whose interest in wind turbines had waned, the German and Danish governments saw wind power as a good energy policy and a way to boost domestic manufacturing jobs. During the 1990s, most of the world's wind turbines were built in Germany and Denmark. By 2008, Denmark had achieved its goal of generating 20 percent of its energy needs from the wind.[4]

Concern over climate change and the depletion of fossil fuels renewed interest in US wind energy in the 1990s. In 1992, Congress passed the Energy Policy Act, which included a new tax

>>

Hundreds of turbines were installed in the hills of Altamont Pass, California, by 1983.

credit to encourage alternative energy production, including wind power. However, a price drop in the late 1990s made natural gas more attractive as a power source and put a damper on wind projects.

It took individual states to get the US wind industry going again. Certain states created standards requiring small percentages of renewable energy to be included in the electricity they purchased. The new standards and tax credits helped spur the US wind industry into a period of

WIND ENERGY TIMELINE

1700 BCE:	First record of a windmill in Mesopotamia
700–900 CE:	Vertical-axis windmill used in Persia
1100:	Horizontal post windmill in use in Europe
1300:	Tower and smock mills used throughout Europe
1887:	First known electricity-generating wind turbine built in Scotland by James Blyth
1888:	American Charles Brush constructs first large-scale wind turbine
1941:	World's first megawatt-sized turbine built in Vermont
1973:	Wind power research and industry spurred by world oil crisis
1980:	First wind farm installed in New Hampshire
1990s:	Wind turbines reach multi-megawatt capacity
2011:	World's most powerful onshore wind turbine (7.5 megawatts) built in Germany

growth, which continues in the first two decades of the twenty-first century. Still, growth of wind power depends on more than tax credits. For wind power to flourish as an alternative energy source, developers must first understand the basic patterns of the wind and the logistics of capturing it.

State standards and tax credits led to renewed interest in wind energy at the turn of the twenty-first century.

CHAPTER 3

ASSESSING THE WIND

Wind is created from solar energy. As the sun heats the earth, it does so unevenly, creating areas of high and low pressure in the atmosphere. The resulting movement of high pressure to low pressure is wind. The earth's features—such as bodies of water, mountains, hills, ridges, and valleys—influence the wind's speed and direction. Elevation also has an influence: wind gets faster, more consistent, and less dense with higher elevation. In order to most effectively capture wind power to produce electricity, engineers must take these factors into consideration. Whether someone is investing in a rooftop turbine for personal use or installing a 200-turbine wind farm, choosing the right site is crucial. Without an understanding of global and local effects on the speed, strength, and consistency of wind, a turbine can turn into a very expensive sculpture.

« **Researchers must take many factors into consideration when seeking out the best location for wind turbine installations.**

GLOBAL WINDS

As the sun heats the planet, some areas warm more quickly than others. For example, Mexico, which is close to the equator, receives more of the sun's energy than Canada, which is closer to the North Pole. Cold air is denser than warm air and it sinks, increasing pressure in the atmosphere. The air from the cool, high-pressure poles constantly moves toward the warm, low-pressure equator. At the same time, the warm air at the equator rises, cools, and flows toward the poles. The resulting air movements between equator and poles are the global winds.

Rather than blowing straight north and south, global winds swerve as Earth spins. This is called the Coriolis effect. In the Northern Hemisphere, winds blowing toward the poles swerve northeast, and winds blowing toward the equator swerve southwest.

LOCAL WINDS AND GEOGRAPHY

Winds are also affected by local changes in air temperature and air pressure. These local changes are caused by uneven warming from the sun and an area's geographic features. One example is a lake breeze or sea breeze. During the day, water absorbs the sun's warmth less quickly than the land. The result is high pressure over the cool water, which moves air—in the form of a breeze—toward land. The effect is reversed at night as the land releases its warmth more quickly than the water and a breeze blows from land toward the lake or ocean.

Air moving between the poles and the equator swerves due to Earth's rotation.

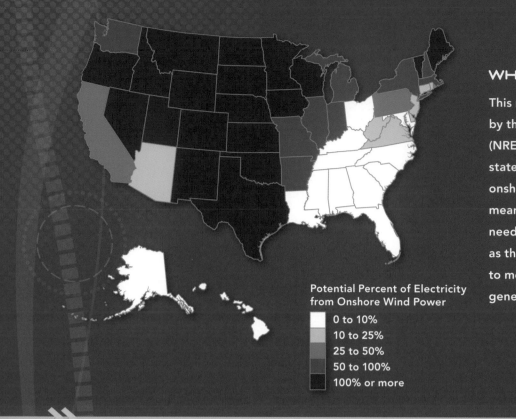

WHERE THE WIND IS

This map, based from information provided by the National Renewable Energy Laboratory (NREL) in 2010, shows how much potential each state has to produce all of its electricity from onshore wind. A figure of 100 percent would mean the state can potentially provide all of its needed electricity with wind. Some states—such as those in the Great Plains—have enough wind to meet their own needs and provide wind-generated electricity to other states.[1]

Potential Percent of Electricity from Onshore Wind Power

- 0 to 10%
- 10 to 25%
- 25 to 50%
- 50 to 100%
- 100% or more

Similarly, the sides of a mountain heat up during the day, warming the air along the bottom and sides of its neighboring valley more than the air in the center of the valley. By the afternoon of a sunny day, warm air is rushing up the sides of the mountain, sped along by cool upper air sinking to the valley floor. After the sun goes down, the land gives up its warmth more quickly than the atmosphere, and cooling air sinks along the mountain's slopes toward the valley floor.

Wind farms near Palm Springs, California, take advantage of winds created by nearby mountains.

SEASONS AND TIME OF DAY

The time of day affects the amount of available wind. In most locations, it is windier during the day than at night due to greater daytime differences in air temperature and, therefore, air pressure. This works in a wind turbine's favor, since more electricity is generally needed during the day than at night.

The temperature of the season influences the wind as well. In the United States, wind tends to be weakest during the warmest months. Knowing the times when wind will be slowest helps wind energy planners predict how much backup energy will be required during those times. Seasonal regional winds—such as the Santa Ana winds in Southern California or the Chinook winds of the Rocky Mountains—can also be utilized for wind energy. But these winds can also pose a danger to turbines if they are not designed to handle occasional onslaughts.

MEASURING WIND SPEED AND STRENGTH

How is it determined if there is enough wind somewhere to keep a turbine spinning? A good indicator is to take a look around for evidence of wind. Are trees bent, or do you notice more branches on one side of the trunk than the other? Are there sand dunes or exposed rocks?

The next step is measuring the area's wind speed, direction, and strength for at least a year. This is usually done with the help of devices called anemometers, but lasers and sonar can also be used to calculate wind speed and direction. A basic anemometer is mounted at varying heights on tall towers, and it usually has three plastic or metal cups that spin on a shaft in the wind. The shaft powers a generator, which creates an electric current. The amount of electricity produced is recorded on a device and translated into miles, kilometers, or knots per hour. The ideal discovery would be that wind speed steadily increases with height, there is a prevailing wind direction, and the amount of wind increases during the day when there is peak demand for electricity. Computer software can then help with spacing and laying out turbines for the best performance.

Some of the most successful wind farms take advantage of more than one local wind effect. For example, turbines in the San Gorgonio Pass near Palm Springs, California, are fed by cool air from the coast that then rushes up a channeled pass toward the desert.

FACTORS AFFECTING WIND SPEED AND STRENGTH

Wind is slowed and made turbulent by natural and man-made obstacles, including trees and shrubs, hills, mountains, buildings, and even rough ground. This is why wind is strongest over flat and open plains and coastal areas over vast expanses of ocean. However, natural channels—such as the valleys between hills, mountains, and canyons—cause winds to compress and speed up, which can be helpful in utilizing wind for energy. Many other factors affect wind speed and strength as well.

Air density affects wind strength. As a substance, air is lighter than water because its molecules are not packed as tightly together. But air density is not consistent, as water density is. Air becomes less dense at higher temperatures or at higher elevations. For example, the air density at 5,000 feet (1,524 m) is approximately 15 percent less than at sea level.[2] Because heavier, denser air packs more of a punch, it provides more power to wind turbines. Thus, air captured from lower elevations or from lower temperatures can provide more power. Turbines in the Arctic have burned out because the power of the cold, sea-level air was more than the turbine could handle.

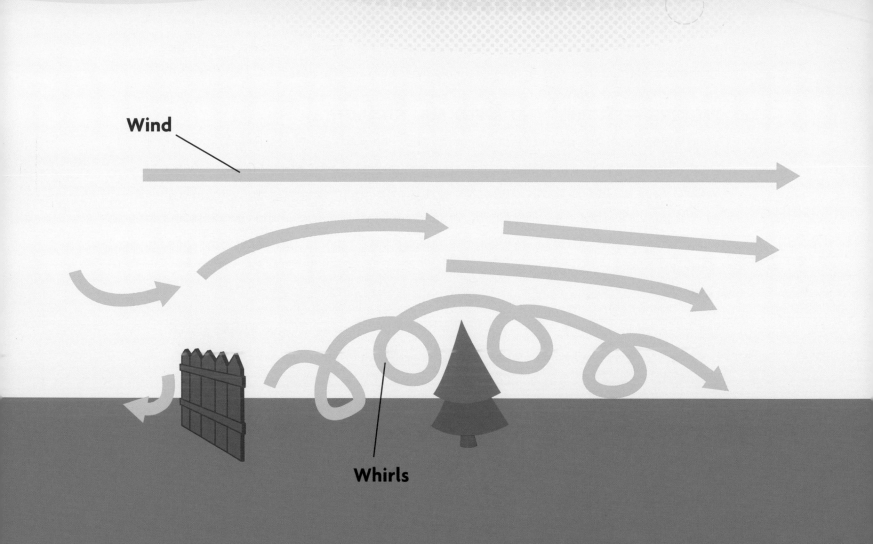

Because air molecules are spaced closer together nearer the earth's surface and there are more objects that interfere with the wind's progress, there is more air friction closer to the ground than higher up. This means air moves slower at lower altitudes than at higher altitudes. Because buildings and landscape features can slow the wind, having tall turbine towers is more critical in hilly terrain than on open plains. The difference in height between the tip of a turbine blade at its highest position and at its lowest position can be hundreds of feet, so it is important that the turbine be tall enough that air speed and quality are the same at both heights.

Air turbulence, or quick changes in the speed and direction of the wind, is created when the wind passes over and around man-made and natural objects. Turbulence slows the wind, and gusty whirls can cause turbine fatigue. Turbine towers need to be tall enough to get out of turbulence zones. They also need to be spaced far enough apart on wind farms so they do not cause turbulence for other wind turbines.

So, after taking all these factors into consideration, it might seem a turbine is ready to be installed. However, assessing wind conditions is only part of the task of implementing a wind energy project. The next step is determining which type of turbine will best capture wind at a chosen site.

**≪ Man-made and natural objects
can create air turbulence.**

CHAPTER 4

TURBINE TYPES

Wind turbines have been developed to maximize every wind condition and location. Most wind turbines today fall under two categories: horizontal axis and vertical axis. Both categories come in varying sizes.

HORIZONTAL-AXIS WIND TURBINE

The horizontal-axis wind turbine is the most common wind turbine in use today. You can think of this turbine as a reverse fan—rather than electricity turning the fan's blades and creating wind, wind turns the turbine's blades, making electricity. While some horizontal-axis turbines may have only one or two blades, most have three blades for greater balance, less vibration, and less noise. Horizontal-axis turbines consist of several basic parts. First is a vertical tower, which can be an enclosed tube or open and grid-like. The tower holds the nacelle. The nacelle is a box-like structure, usually made of

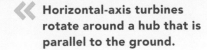

Horizontal-axis turbines rotate around a hub that is parallel to the ground.

fiberglass. The nacelle houses additional mechanical components of the turbine. The nacelle also holds the rotor, which consists of the blades and central hub, or nose, together. The hub anchors the blades and is horizontal to the ground. The blades rotate around it. The entire rotor (blades and hub) faces into the wind.

Power is generated when the wind's force turns the turbine's rotor. The rotor spins, which turns a rod, or shaft, that feeds into a gearbox inside the nacelle. Using multiple wheels and bearings, the gearbox converts the speed of the turning blade—typically 15 to 20 rotations per minute for a one-megawatt turbine—into 1,800 rotations per minute, the speed needed to create electricity. A shaft from the gearbox feeds into a generator. Using magnetic fields, the generator converts the rotational energy it receives from the gearbox shaft into electric voltage, measured in watts. The electric voltage from the generator travels through a wire to a transformer, which is either inside the nacelle, in or on the tower, or in a separate structure on the ground. The transformer converts the power to the right voltage needed to feed into an electric grid. Then electricity from the grid is sent to power homes and businesses.

WIND TURBINE WATTS

Watts are the units used to measure the power potential of wind and wind turbines. An average lightbulb has anywhere from 25 to 150 watts. One kilowatt can power ten 100-watt lightbulbs. One thousand kilowatts make up one megawatt. Energy output is measured in watt-hours. For example:

> One kilowatt-hour is enough to operate one 40-watt lightbulb for a full day.[1]
> A one-megawatt wind turbine operating at full capacity for one hour would produce one megawatt-hour of electricity.[2]
> One megawatt-hour will power approximately 1,000 homes for one day.[3]

Small wind turbines might not connect to a grid. If the turbine does not connect to a utility grid, it does not require transformers. It does, however, use batteries so excess electricity can be stored and used when the wind isn't blowing. On top of the nacelle, devices measure wind direction and speed. Underneath, another device swivels the nacelle so it is always facing the wind. Rotors in commercial turbine models also include technology that can turn each blade to best catch the wind. Most commercial wind turbine nacelles also house an emergency brake to stop the rotor in dangerous high winds or for technician safety.

VERTICAL-AXIS WIND TURBINE

The blades of a vertical-axis wind turbine rotate around a vertical shaft, similar to a carousel. The two types of vertical-axis turbines in use today are the Darrieus and the Savonius. Invented in France in the 1920s and patented in 1931, the Darrieus resembles an eggbeater standing on end. Its long, curved blades extend from the top to the bottom of a long shaft. Variations of the Darrieus include the Giromill, which has shorter, straighter blades. The Savonius, invented in Finland in 1922, is a simple vertical-axis turbine with scooped blades that resemble sections of a tube or a pipe cut in half. The long ends of the two or three blades are attached to a vertical shaft and catch the wind like boat sails.

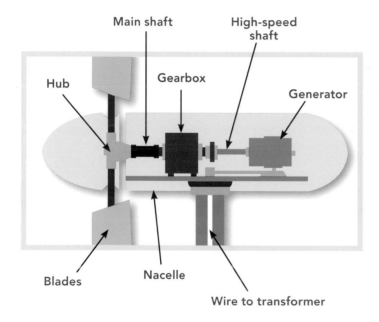

Main shaft

High-speed shaft

Hub

Gearbox

Generator

Blades

Nacelle

Wire to transformer

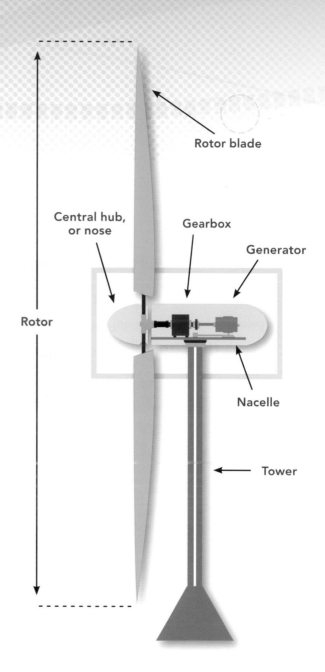

Rotor blade

Central hub, or nose

Gearbox

Generator

Rotor

Nacelle

Tower

HORIZONTAL-AXIS WIND TURBINE

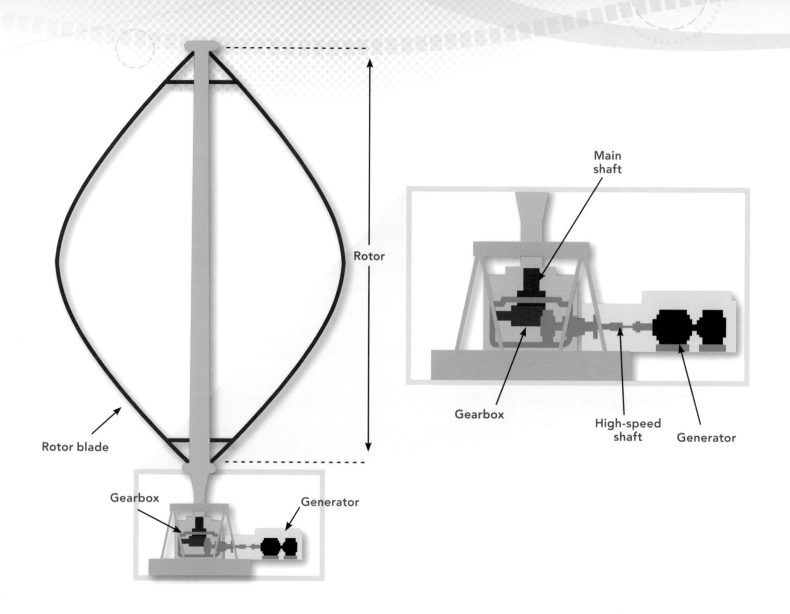

Rotor

Rotor blade

Gearbox

Generator

Main
shaft

Gearbox

High-speed
shaft

Generator

VERTICAL–AXIS WIND TURBINE

A vertical-axis Darrieus turbine, *left*, and a vertical-axis Savonius turbine, *right*.

Vertical-axis turbines share the same basic operating principles as horizontal-axis turbines: wind turns the blades and a rotor, which spins a shaft that feeds into a gearbox. The high-speed output shaft from the gearbox feeds into a generator, which creates electric voltage. The electricity then passes into the electric grid via a transformer or into a battery. The main difference between the two is the way the blades rotate around the axis.

WHICH TURBINE TYPE IS BEST?

The main difference between horizontal- and vertical-axis turbines is configuration. In horizontal-axis turbines, the gearbox and generator are located in a nacelle attached to the turning rotor. In vertical-axis turbines, the gearbox and generator are located beneath the rotor. The rotor includes the blades and the nose they are attached to. The rotor on vertical-axis turbines spins around a vertical shaft. Another difference is how wind moves the blades. Blades are shaped to act like airplane wings. When wind passes over a blade, a pocket of low pressure forms on the other side, pulling the blade toward the low pressure. This effect is called lift. The force of wind against the front of the blade is called drag. While turbines use both lift and drag to turn the rotor, lift is a much stronger and more efficient force.

The configuration of horizontal-axis turbines makes them more efficient than their vertical-axis counterparts. A portion of a vertical-axis rotor is always turning against the wind's force,

LIFT AND DRAG

Lift is the upward force of the wind. Drag is the force exerted by air (or other gas or a liquid) against and around a moving object. The effects of lift and drag are used in wind turbines and airplane wings. In lift, wind passing over a blade creates low pressure on the opposite side. The blade is pulled toward the low pressure. Drag is the force of the wind pushing against the blade.

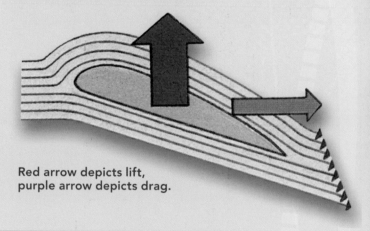

Red arrow depicts lift, purple arrow depicts drag.

whereas a horizontal-axis rotor always faces the wind and turns with the wind's force. As a result, vertical-axis turbines are not as widely used as horizontal-axis turbines. However, they are a good choice in special situations. For example, vertical-axis turbines can often handle turbulence better than horizontal turbines, often making them ideal for areas with extreme and variable weather. They also tend to be quieter, which makes them popular in cities and suburbs. Due to the high efficiency—and resulting high energy output—of horizontal-axis turbines, these remain the choice for most commercial wind applications.

Wind is quickly growing as a source of electricity. As of 2010, wind energy contributed 2.9 percent of all electricity consumed in the United States.[4] That percentage will likely keep rising as turbine technology improves.

Vertical-axis and horizontal-axis turbines each have advantages and disadvantages to consider for maximum efficiency in particular locations or conditions.

CHAPTER 5

BENEFITS OF WIND ENERGY

I n contrast to fossil fuels, wind energy is a plentiful energy source that will never run out. Wind is easily found—no digging, mining, or excavating required. And wind does not pollute the atmosphere or generate hazardous waste.

CLEAN AND LOW IMPACT

In fact, wind is one of the cleanest sources of energy in use today. It has been estimated that if only 10 percent of US wind potential was tapped to produce energy, total US carbon dioxide emissions would fall by 33 percent.[1]

Wind energy is also proving its worth. For example, Texas was the number one producer of wind energy in the United States in 2011.[2] As one *National Review* journalist said of West Texas, "So persistent is the wind that a legend has it that it stopped blowing once for half a minute and all the chickens fell over between Amarillo and San

« As opposed to fossil fuel power plants that emit pollutants, producing electricity by wind energy is a clean process.

Angelo."[3] Wind farms in Texas helped prevent blackouts during the state's record heat wave and drought. Unlike coal, gas, or nuclear energy, wind energy does not require water in any of its stages of production.

COST

Wind energy saves on the hidden costs associated with conventional energy sources, such as trade deficits, the environmental costs of depleted resources, and the health and environmental costs of pollution. A study by the European Environment Agency found that pollution from the use of fossil fuels is expensive as well as harmful. Costs in Europe associated with health care, loss of productivity, crop losses, and other damage from pollution amounted to more than $130 billion in 2009.[4]

According to financial news organization Bloomberg, the cost of wind electricity is expected to fall by 12 percent by 2016.[5] There are a few reasons for the likely drop: manufacturers keep getting better at making turbines, materials keep improving, larger and more efficient turbines lower per-kilowatt costs, and operators are gaining more experience with plant operations and maintenance. It is also anticipated that as more manufacturers get into the wind business, there will be an abundance of turbines on the market, which will further reduce costs. If wind systems are mass-produced in the future, costs will drop even more.

Engineers are becoming better equipped to maintain today's large turbines, making them more efficient and more cost-effective.

Turbines can successfully coexist with livestock and crops.

According to an article by George Washington University's GW Solar Institute, the cost of wind energy in 2010 was approximately 7.5 cents per kilowatt-hour. According to the same article, natural gas was approximately 6.4 cents per kilowatt-hour and coal was approximately 8 cents per kilowatt-hour in 2010.[6] By these estimations, wind power was relatively competitive with conventional energy sources. If costs for wind energy drop as much as Bloomberg's analysts believe, average US onshore wind electricity will be as cheap as natural gas by 2016.[7]

In addition to lowered cost predictions, wind turbines can bring needed tax revenue to local communities and yield extra income for landowners. Some of the strongest wind-producing areas in the United States stretch across the Midwest and Great Plains, where farmers and rural landowners are installing wind turbines and selling the excess power for profit. Landowners are also leasing land to wind farm developers. Because a large turbine typically takes up less than 0.5 acre (0.2 ha), a farmer can plant crops around it and animals can graze close to the base of the tower.

A POPULAR ENERGY CHOICE

Wind energy is environmentally friendly and cost competitive. It creates jobs, boosts the economy, and promotes national security. What's not to like? Not much, polls suggest. The American Wind Energy Association (AWEA) published results of a 2010 study stating, "89 percent of

JUST HOW POPULAR IS WIND POWER?

In a March 2011 CNN/Opinion Research Corporation poll, 83 percent of respondents believed wind power should be relied on more for the United States's energy needs, versus 17 percent who believed it should be relied on less.[8] A March 2011 poll by consulting company Gallup asked, "Which of the following approaches to solving the nation's energy problems do you think the US should follow right now?" At 66 percent to 26 percent, respondents preferred the development of alternative energy—such as wind and solar power—to the production of more oil, gas, and coal power.[9]

RENEWABLE ENERGY CREDITS

Most US states with renewable energy standards or mandates allow utilities—usually electric utilities—to trade renewable energy credits (RECs) with other utilities. A renewable-energy facility—such as a commercial wind farm—earns RECs for every kilowatt- or megawatt-hour of electricity it produces each year. Those RECs can be bought and sold by utilities that need to comply with mandates. If utilities do not own enough renewable energy sources—such as wind farms—to meet requirements, they can purchase RECs. While some might consider this cheating, RECs create a competitive market for renewable energy, which helps drive down costs.

American voters believe increasing the amount of energy the nation gets from wind is a good idea."[10]

Politically, alternative energies are often seen as appealing more to liberal than conservative voters. But wind is a renewable power that crosses party lines. In August 2011, a coalition of 24 US Republican and Democrat governors asked the Obama administration to extend both the Production Tax Credit (PTC), which provides a tax credit for electricity from a utility-scale turbine's first ten years, and the Investment Tax Credit, which allows taxpayers to receive a tax credit reimbursing a percentage of renewable energy purchase and installation, each for seven years. In their letter to the president, they also requested that he expand wind energy programs and ease rules for offshore wind development. The outlook for wind power appears positive. However, various social, political, and economic issues may hinder future wind power growth.

Many believe in wind power as a positive step toward a clean energy future.

DRAWBACKS OF WIND ENERGY

No energy source is perfect, including the wind. Some drawbacks stem from the nature of wind itself, while others arise from the technology that turns wind into electricity. Whatever the challenge, wind energy experts are working on innovations that address these issues.

INTERMITTENT ENERGY

By its nature, wind continuously changes speed, and at times, it stops altogether. This means even utilities with a lot of wind-generated electricity need backup energy systems, such as coal- and gas-burning power plants. Firing up fossil fuel plants on demand can be inefficient and expensive. To deal with intermittent winds, wind farm operators are trying to get better at predicting peak and low wind periods.

 When the wind stops blowing, conventional power plants take over creating energy.

The US Department of Energy's National Renewable Energy Laboratory (NREL) argues that intermittent winds will be less of a problem as more wind farms are built around the country and fed into a common grid.[1] The wind is always blowing somewhere, so many turbines averaged over a large area will increase the minimum amount of available energy.

Rather than sending electricity directly from turbines into the grid, it has also been suggested that wind turbine energy be stored for later use. New battery technologies include General Electric's (GE) Zebra battery, which uses molten salt and gets blazing hot, providing a higher energy density. Other storage ideas include converting wind energy into compressed air or hydrogen that can later be turned into electricity.

NOT IN MY BACKYARD

Where good winds blow, transmission lines are not always around to get the electricity where it is needed. However, when locations with prime wind conditions and proper transmission lines are found, residents in those areas can introduce further complications. Some people support wind energy in general but do not want turbines in their own neighborhood. Opposition by residents to local developments is sometimes called *NIMBY*, which stands for "not in my backyard." Several factors can contribute to the NIMBY view. Gripes about the unsightliness of wind turbines have dogged the wind industry for as long as wind farms have existed. A turbine

A turbine towers over a field, casting a massive shadow.

rotor with the diameter of a football field is impossible to ignore, as is the looming shadow that flickers at one end. When a turbine shadow lands on a home or business, the flickering caused by rotating wind turbine blades is annoying for some. Using landscaping to block the shadows and stopping turbines at certain times of the day are two solutions. Some communities also have laws limiting turbine flicker.

Some residents living close to wind turbines complain that the low-frequency sounds and vibrations they emit cause physical problems, including rapid heartbeat, nausea, and blurred vision. While evidence does not seem to support a connection between turbines and these health problems, the annoyance factor of turbine noise is a real issue. Of the 250 new US wind farms that went online in 2009 and 2010, approximately 12 generated significant noise complaints.[2]

ACCEPTABLE DECIBELS

Many states set limits on nighttime noise. In Maine, for example, the limit is 45 decibels, which is about the same level of noise as a humming refrigerator.[3] A normal conversation is approximately 60 decibels.[4] From approximately a quarter of a mile (0.4 km) away, the sound of a typical commercial horizontal-axis wind turbine is between 35 to 45 decibels.[5]

While some sound comes from the moving parts inside the nacelle, the biggest culprit is the swooshing sound made as the turbine blades slice though the air. Most current turbines are built with systems to dampen blade noise. Some noise is masked by the wind itself, and when the wind is not blowing, the machine does not operate and is quiet. Other fixes include placing turbines as far from residential neighborhoods as possible and turning turbines off at night when people are trying to sleep.

Others may oppose wind power because of the subsidies it receives, or because it is owned by big multinational corporations. Additionally, some wind implementation projects are just poorly executed. They are proposed in locations too close to homes or near sensitive habitats.

THREATS TO WILDLIFE

It has long been a concern that wind turbines pose a threat to birds. In 2001, the US National Wind Coordinating Committee (NWCC) reported that the 15,000 US wind turbines in operation at the time killed 33,000 birds every year, or 2.2 birds per turbine per year.[6] Wind turbines can be especially deadly to endangered species—including eagles, hawks, and other raptors—that hunt in the open areas where wind farms are often located.

However, while the number of bird fatalities caused by turbines is certainly troubling, it is just a fraction of the hundreds of millions of birds killed every year. The goal in preventing

turbine-related deaths is to decrease turbine-animal contact. A big effort toward this goal is paying close attention to turbine placement. The US Fish and Wildlife Service (FWS) recommends potential wind sites be carefully studied and avoided if they conflict with migration patterns or critical bird habitats. The FWS is also looking into the use of commercial vertical-axis turbines, which are lower to the ground and more bird friendly. Some organizations, including the US Geological Survey, have raised concerns over a high number of bat deaths related to wind turbines.[8] Slowing the rotor speed and painting the blades with a pattern may make turbines easier to see and prevent bird and bat deaths. It has also been suggested that wind farms be shut down during low wind, which is also when bats are most active.

RADAR AND TELECOMMUNICATION INTERFERENCE

Because wind turbines are tall and have moving blades, they can be mistaken for airplanes on radar. At their worst, wind farms can swamp sensitive radar with images. This creates a confusing mess on the screen called a black

WIND TURBINES AND BATS

More bats than birds are killed every year by wind turbines, but only half die from collisions.[9] Because bats use sound to navigate, they are better than birds at avoiding twirling wind turbine blades. But bats cannot detect the area of low pressure that forms behind the rotor. When they fly into this area, the bats' internal airways rapidly expand. The resulting internal bleeding causes half of all turbine-related bat deaths.[10]

 It can be hard for birds to avoid spinning turbine blades when flying past.

hole, which makes it almost impossible to track aircraft. In addition to radar interference, wind turbines can disrupt a ship's onboard navigational instruments. This is an especially big concern for countries with offshore wind farms.

Researchers have been experimenting with methods to make wind turbines less intrusive to radar technology. One promising technique includes incorporating material that absorbs radar energy into turbine blades as they are built. The blades, nacelle, and tower can also be sprayed with the special material. Other fixes include altering radar software and hardware so the radar essentially ignores wind turbines. The US Department of Homeland Security is funding research to help wind farm developers determine if a project will interfere with radar sites.

BLADE EFFICIENCY

Current blade length for a turbine is limited to approximately 500 feet (152 m) due to heavy weight and flexing. Power is proportional to the area of the circle made by the blades. Increasing the blade length means the circle's radius is increased and more power is generated. In order to reach a wind industry goal of 800-foot (244 m) blades by 2020, manufacturers are experimenting with lighter and tougher blade materials, including polyurethane reinforced with nanotubes.[11] Nanotubes are tiny, light cylindrical structures made of carbon. The resulting

»
Too much weight and flexing can lead to turbine blade damage.

material is eight times tougher and substantially lighter and more rigid than the fiberglass used in typical wind turbine blades.[12]

Current turbine blades can flex up to 20 feet (6 m) in strong gusts, creating vibration and stress to the machine. One company is experimenting with shooting puffs of air along the length of the blade to disrupt the natural airflow of gusts. Other companies are testing flaps along the trailing edge of the blade, such as the ones found on airplane wings, to change the blade's aerodynamics to better match wind conditions. Flaps have the added benefit of reducing turbine noise.

"There is nothing nostalgic or romantic about them. They represent not the pioneer past but an uncertain future. The turbines evoke feelings of technophobia. They are steel and they are massive. . . . Visually, they seem to rival nature rather than cooperate with it."[13]—**Robert W. Righter, author of** *Wind Energy in America: A History*, **describing today's larger wind turbines**

TRANSPORTATION

Utility-scale wind turbines can be big. Really big. Turbines continue to grow because larger turbines are more efficient and cost-effective. As a result, 2.5-megawatt and 3-megawatt units are becoming more common. The nacelles, blades, and shafts of these towers—which can reach 60 to 70 feet (18 to 21 m) in length, 15 feet (5 m) in diameter, and weigh 10,000 to 150,000 pounds (4,500 to 68,000 kg)—require special transportation equipment and routes, and they have to comply with state Department of Transportation requirements.[14] All of this means added costs and delays, especially if routes cross state lines.

ELECTRICITY TRANSMISSION AND LIMITED LOCATIONS

A potential wind farm site can encounter snags if no existing transmission lines are nearby or the site has old lines that need to be modernized to meet the demands of wind electricity. Many countries are making progress planning for new power lines, and this progress will continue into the future. In addition to the 11,900 miles (19,150 km) of new or under-construction lines in the United States in 2010, it is projected that an additional 39,000 miles (62,800 km) will be installed by 2020, according to a 2010 Wind Technologies Market Report by the US Department of Energy.[15] For coastal areas of the United States, offshore wind farms may provide a solution to this. These wind farms, installed in bodies of water rather than on land, can be stationed close to major cities where there is a market for electricity.

For future wind implementation, placement is key. Choosing a good site can mean the difference between wind energy success and failure. The social and environmental drawbacks of wind turbines, such as visual and noise pollution, bird deaths, and radar interference need to be fully studied before a potential wind site gets a green light. Questions wind developers might want to consider include:

- How close will the turbines be to homes and businesses?

- Are local residents in favor of, or opposed to, the project?

- Are there any endangered birds using the area, or is the site part of a migratory path?

- Are there any military installations or airports nearby that use radar?

- Are there sufficient transmission lines nearby?

- Which local, regional, and state laws affect the project, and what kinds of approvals and permits are needed?

There are many successfully functioning wind turbine sites around the world. One way these sites produce maximum results is through placement of several turbines together on wind farms.

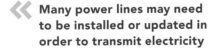

Many power lines may need to be installed or updated in order to transmit electricity from future wind turbines.

ONSHORE WIND: WIND FARMS

A wind farm is a group of wind turbines placed near each other that together supply energy to a utility grid. A wind farm can be anything from a few wind turbines that collectively power a home to hundreds of turbines funneling electricity into a national grid. Wind farms at sea and in the air are currently being developed, but onshore wind farms, or wind farms on land, are the most common wind farms in use today.

ONSHORE WIND BENEFITS AND CHALLENGES

Wind farms are an efficient way to gather the maximum amount of wind in an area. Most turbines are not constantly in rotation from wind. One turbine may stop rotating due to insufficient wind while another one in the distance is getting hit with a gust. A large wind farm with multiple turbines is more likely to have at least one turbine catching wind at all times. Modern turbines create electricity approximately 70 to 85 percent of the

« **Wind farms make use of prime wind locations such as this open hillside.**

time, though not always at full capacity. Because wind is intermittent, turbines typically produce at approximately 30 percent capacity.[1] Location affects capacity, and offshore wind turbine capacity can be higher than onshore capacity.

Large onshore wind farms can stretch for miles. Each turbine must be placed far enough apart to avoid blades hitting each other. Areas with unobstructed space and strong winds are usually the best sites. Onshore wind farm developers often investigate mountainsides, prairies, and fields as potential farm sites. The fields of actual farms are often used, as turbines can coexist alongside crops or livestock.

Wind developers who find prime locations for wind farms often face many challenges before development can happen. Planners must consider the shadows the tall towers cast, the air turbulence spinning blades create for other turbines nearby, and the farm's proximity to an electric grid. How much energy the turbines will

WIND FARMS ON FARMS

Constant rotation of a turbine blade can change the temperature of the surrounding air, according to the US Department of Energy's Ames Laboratory in Iowa.[2] This temperature change can be both beneficial and damaging to crops that grow on a wind farm. The turning blades can aid growth of corn and soybean crops by keeping them cool during the day, ushering warm air toward them at night, and keeping the plants dry, which prevents infestations. However, this drying effect can be detrimental as well. Crops may become too dry and need to be watered more.

Sweeping, unobstructed expanses of land often make the best onshore wind farm sites.

produce at a given site and for how long must be considered, as does the topography of a site. Developers must study the wind in the area, determine the type of turbine best suited for the area, and then carefully calculate the desired distance between each turbine.

On average, turbines on farms are placed seven rotor diameters apart. That means a turbine with a 300-foot (91 m) rotor should be placed 2,100 feet (640 m) away from another turbine the same size. However, a 2011 study by Charles Meneveau of Johns Hopkins University in Maryland and Johan Meyers of Leuven University in Belgium suggests placing turbines a greater distance apart would be more effective. According to their study, turbine blades distort the wind around them, creating turbulence that can affect nearby turbines. This turbulence can be a good thing if the proper spacing is applied. Turbulence created from calculated spacing can stir the air and help the turbines draw on the powerful wind found at higher altitudes. Using wind tunnel experiments and computer simulations, Meneveau and Meyers calculated that 15 rotor diameters—more than double what is commonly in practice—is optimal spacing.[3]

A groundbreaking design from biophysicist John Dabiri aims to turn wind turbine proximity on a wind farm into an asset rather than a constraint. Instead of placing his vertical-axis turbines far apart, Dabiri sites them close together so each turbine is powered by its neighbor's turbulence. He says the pattern produces ten times as much power in the same amount of space, per square meter of land, taken up by horizontal-axis turbines on wind farms.[5] As of 2011, Dabiri was field-testing his turbines in Southern California.

TURBINE SIZE

Today's wind turbines are big. They can generate 50 times more electricity than turbines that graced the hills of the Altamont Pass, California, in the 1980s.[6] As of 2011, the largest onshore wind turbine was a 7.5-megawatt, 440-foot (134 m) giant built by German company Enercon. Wind turbines are growing taller to access stronger winds at higher altitudes. Turbine blades

**Turbines today are
mammoth compared to
older versions, meaning
onshore wind farm
area must be greater.**

are also growing longer because longer blades produce more power. Larger turbines with
innovative materials can equal lower costs according to Wind Measurement International, which
states,

> Because newer turbines are usually quite substantially larger you get an economy of
> scale, lower maintenance costs per [kilowatt] of rated power. This is simply because you
> do not need to service a large turbine any more often than a small one. Couple this with

the constant development of new materials and techniques and you will make savings on the maintenance costs.[7]

While most commercial turbine manufacturers continue to head in a bigger-is-better direction, size has its drawbacks. In addition to each individual turbine being more expensive and difficult to transport, large onshore turbines typically need to be spaced up to one mile (1.6 km) apart to avoid turbulence from other turbines.[8] Finding wind farm areas with enough available land and perfect wind conditions can be difficult.

Several innovations address the physical issues of onshore wind farm implementation. Three French designers are touting vertical-axis turbines that fit inside existing high-voltage electric towers, which means they wouldn't take up any additional space. Called Wind-it turbines, these models could be plugged directly into an electric grid and, if implemented in the United States, take advantage of the country's thousands of miles of high-voltage lines that cross windy fields and ridges. As of 2009, the developers of the Wind-it turbine had a scale model and were looking for an industrial partner.

Another new turbine, the FloDesign, was inspired by jet engines. Funnel-like cylinders that suck in wind and direct it to a fast-spinning rotor surround this horizontal-axis turbine. The inventors claim the turbine can harness three to four times more power than typical commercial turbines, and they can be placed closer together because they disturb less air.[9]

REVENUE AND SUBSIDIES

Potential revenue is an important aspect of wind farm installation. Investors want to feel confident that a wind farm will make money once it is up and running. This means the turbines need to perform as expected and the price of wind energy needs to be competitive with other energy sources. If the prices of conventional energy sources, such as coal and gas, are high, developers

TAX CREDITS

The PTC was implemented in 1992 as part of the Energy Policy Act. Adjusted for inflation, the PTC provided a tax credit of 2.2 cents per kilowatt-hour in 2011 for the production of electricity from utility-scale wind turbines.[10] Since its beginning, the PTC has gone through four extensions and was allowed to die out three times. This on-again, off-again nature has contributed to boom-and-bust fluctuations in the wind industry, as represented in the graph.

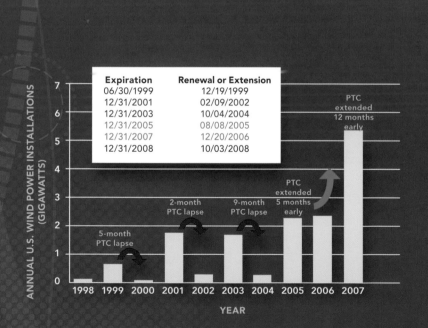

Expiration	Renewal or Extension
06/30/1999	12/19/1999
12/31/2001	02/09/2002
12/31/2003	10/04/2004
12/31/2005	08/08/2005
12/31/2007	12/20/2006
12/31/2008	10/03/2008

*Source: Electricity from Renewable Resources: Status, Prospects, and Impediments. National Academies Press

are more likely to take a chance on wind. But fuel prices fluctuate. In 2009, for example, new natural gas deposits were discovered in the United States that hold enough fuel to potentially last more than 100 years.[11] Partly as a result of this news, the price of natural gas dropped, making wind energy a less appealing investment.

Federal financial subsidies help stimulate wind-energy projects. Federal financial subsidies are grants given by the government to aid a project considered beneficial to the public. These subsidies provided to wind-energy projects come primarily in the form of tax incentives and research grants.

As of 2010, 37 US states and the District of Columbia had renewable portfolio standards or mandates. These are formal policies requiring electricity providers to include a certain portion of their power from renewable sources. To comply with mandates, some providers might import renewable electricity into the state or trade RECs with other utilities. Tax incentives and a supportive political atmosphere can help sway investors toward backing wind projects, but concerns about public opposition and tax incentives running out can also frighten investors away.

Energy mandates and exciting innovations project a positive outlook on addressing the challenges of onshore wind farms. For many countries, however, the answer to harnessing big wind lies in the sea.

BIG WIND: WIND FARMS AT SEA

In all of Europe, 800 offshore wind turbines were in operation in 2011.[1] No offshore wind farms were operating in the United States that year, but at least one project was in the works. The Cape Wind project in Nantucket Sound, Massachusetts, was the first offshore project to receive all necessary permits to begin installation.[2] As planned, 130 turbines will provide 75 percent of the electricity needs for Cape Cod, Martha's Vineyard, and Nantucket.[3] Construction was slated to begin in 2013.

OFFSHORE BASICS

Vertical-axis turbines are being designed for use in the sea, but today's offshore wind farms use primarily horizontal-axis turbines. Offshore horizontal-axis wind turbines are much like land-based turbines—a tall tower topped by a nacelle and a three-bladed rotor. The main differences are that electricity flows through cables along the

Offshore turbines are a promising enterprise in future wind power installations.

seabed rather than underground, and more corrosion-resistant materials are used on the tower, nacelle, and blades. Towers are attached to foundations planted in the seabed to ensure the structure can withstand hurricanes and the constant battering of ocean waves. Costs and construction requirements mean the water in which offshore turbines are installed needs to be fairly shallow—typically a maximum depth of approximately 160 feet (50 m).[4] This is why most offshore turbines are built close to shore and can easily be seen from land.

ANCHORED OFFSHORE

One of the biggest advantages of offshore wind is that there are fewer obstacles on the sea slowing the wind down, so it blows steadier and stronger. This equates to a 10 to 20 percent increase in energy production, and with all the open space, turbines can be bigger to take advantage of the extra power.[5] Because large metropolitan areas are often located on coasts, the electricity from offshore turbines usually does not have far to travel to reach existing transmission lines. The power is right where it is needed. Another advantage of offshore wind turbines is ease of transport. Offshore turbines are most often transported with specialized crane vessels and barges that are large but have ample space on the water. Trucks bearing huge blades and sections of towers do not need to cross small rural roads as they do for land-based wind farms.

Offshore wind farms have their share of disadvantages as well. Given the need for larger turbines and underwater foundations, the corrosion problems that can arise, and the challenges of transporting, installing, and maintaining turbines at sea, offshore wind farms can be approximately 30 to 50 percent more expensive than their onshore counterparts.[7] Developers are often still willing to invest in offshore wind farms, however, since the added costs are usually offset by increased energy production. Another big issue with offshore wind farms is public opposition. Similar to many coastal areas, Nantucket is appreciated for its natural beauty, and residents close to the proposed Cape Wind project did not like the idea of giant turbines impeding their ocean views.

POLITICAL SUPPORT FOR OFFSHORE WIND FARMS

In 2011, US Interior Secretary Ken Salazar and Energy Secretary Steven Chu announced the federal government would spend up to $50.5 million through 2016 to make offshore wind farms viable. The money was to be spent on developing new turbine designs, installing hardware, and removing market barriers. Approximately 78 percent of US demand for electricity lies in 28 coastal states, which makes capturing wind energy at sea a logical idea.[8] This especially holds true on the East Coast, where there is less available land and poorer wind conditions for onshore wind farms.

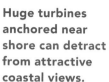

Huge turbines anchored near shore can detract from attractive coastal views.

DEEPER SEA: FLOATING TURBINES

The solution to many offshore wind pitfalls may be taking the technology deeper into the ocean. Deep-sea wind farms have the advantage of being invisible and inaudible from land. Another big plus is that wind is stronger and steadier farther out to sea, meaning turbines can generate even more power. And given that the coasts of many highly populated areas, including Japan, Europe, and the US West Coast, have water that is too deep—over 160 feet (50 m)—for most anchored offshore turbines, turbines that float on the water's surface are a viable choice for taking advantage of offshore wind energy.[9]

In 2009, the Norwegian company StatoilHydro created Hywind, a 2.3-megawatt turbine mounted on a tower that rises 213 feet (65 m) above the water on a floating platform. The platform is tethered off the Norwegian coast by cables buried in the seabed 722 feet (220 m) below the surface. The turbine is successfully adding electricity to the Norwegian grid.

A US wind developer, Principle Power, designed WindFloat, which has a floating foundation that pumps seawater between its three floats to balance the platform and keep it upright. The floating platform and its two-megawatt turbine were deployed at the end of 2011 off the coast of Portugal. Several other companies around the world are currently working on deep-water wind turbine technologies as well.

DOWNSIDES OF FLOATING TURBINES

Floating turbines may seem to solve the problems of offshore turbines, but there are catches. As with traditional offshore turbines, cost is a big factor. Floating turbines need to be big—capable of producing five to ten megawatts—in order to take advantage of strong wind conditions. Larger turbines are more expensive. Maintenance is also more costly, and rough seas or bad weather can limit the number of days technicians are able to access turbines. The large turbines also make weight and stability issues.

However, solutions are being researched for each problem associated with floating turbines. Proven platform technologies from the offshore oil and gas industries—such as moorings and deep hulls with low centers of gravity—could deal with balance. To reduce maintenance trips, innovations such as direct drivetrains are already being implemented for standard offshore turbines. Direct drivetrains eliminate the need for the maintenance-heavy gearbox by feeding the rotor shaft directly into a generator. Additionally, in order to reduce construction and installation costs, floating-turbine developers are designing platforms to assemble the turbines onshore rather than at sea.

ADDRESSING POWER AND MAINTENANCE

GE is working on a new offshore turbine designed to harness more wind while minimizing expensive at-sea repairs. The turbine's 176-foot (54 m) lightweight blades are 40 percent longer than average with a more aerodynamic shape. The blades will sweep an area the size of two football fields. Inside the nacelle, the rotor shaft feeds directly into a generator. This eliminates the need for a gearbox, a turbine component frequently in need of repair. Permanent magnets in the generator replace a slew of other components. The four-megawatt turbine, which is expected to go online in 2012, will capture 25 percent more wind than other offshore models.[10]

The constant battering from waves must be addressed in implementation of all offshore wind turbines, but floating, rather than anchored, turbines are especially vulnerable.

SMALL WIND: HOMES, BUSINESSES, AND COMMUNITIES

Wind turbines are not only designed to generate multiple megawatts of power for utility grids. Microturbines that produce one kilowatt of electricity might power a fence or a streetlight. Small to medium turbines—used alone or in clusters— power individual homes, businesses, and communities. New technologies and innovations are emerging to accommodate rural, urban, and suburban dwellers who want to take advantage of wind-generated electricity as a primary source of power or to supplement power from a utility grid.

HOME AND BUSINESS WIND INSTALLATIONS

According to the AWEA, wind projects of 100 kilowatts or less have increased every year in the United States since 2005, up 29 percent from 2009 to 2010.[1] In addition to lowering monthly electric bills, wind turbine installations are often eligible for tax

 A small turbine on a home roof

WHO OWNS AND BUYS US WIND POWER PROJECTS?

Independent producers own 83 percent of wind power, electric utilities own 15 percent, and community wind projects own 2 percent. In addition to the 15 percent of wind power owned by utility companies, these companies buy 49 percent of all wind-power capacity in the United States. Ultimately, they control a total of 64 percent of all wind power available in the country.[2]

US WIND PROJECT OWNERS

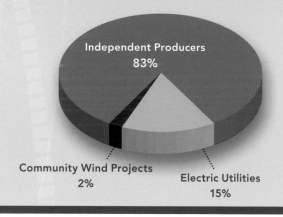

Independent Producers
83%

Community Wind Projects
2%

Electric Utilities
15%

credits, financial rebates, cash incentives, and net metering, a program that credits customers for the excess electricity they produce. For homeowners living off the grid (not connected to public utilities), wind turbines can provide a significant portion of a home's electricity needs.

COMMUNITY WIND INSTALLATIONS

Big corporations own most wind farms. Wind projects owned wholly or in part by local residents and businesses are called community wind. These projects were located primarily in Minnesota, Washington, California, Iowa, and Texas.

In Europe, community wind has long been popular. Community wind was the foundation of the Danish wind industry. Today, nearly 5 percent of Danes own one or more shares in clusters of medium-sized local wind turbines. And in Germany, approximately 200,000 people own shares of local wind turbines.[3]

WEIGHING COMMUNITY WIND

Located high off the ground, roofs seem to be a logical place for wind turbines. However, some consider them an eyesore, and in addition to making noise, a traditional horizontal-axis turbine vibrates as its rotor spins. These vibrations are not good for residents' nerves or for a building's structure. Many innovations are being implemented or researched to address these issues. Promising solutions include vertical-axis turbines and new twists on horizontal-axis designs. Examples of new-generation roof-mounted wind turbines for homes and businesses that are in the production or planning stages include:

NET METERING

People whose homes are connected to an electric grid and who install wind turbines may be able to take advantage of a process called net metering. When a turbine creates more energy than the homeowner needs, the excess electricity is fed into the utility company's electric grid. The home's electric meter spins backward instead of forward, and the credit is applied to the homeowner's next energy bill. As of November 2010, net metering programs were available in 43 states and the District of Columbia. Net metering originated to encourage customers to invest in renewable energy.

For approximately half that price, a number of new companies are selling refurbished turbines. Some of them are from wind farms installed during the 1980s California wind rush. The warranties on revamped machines are not as good as those on new ones, and refurbished turbines require more maintenance. Nonetheless, demand for used turbines is expected to rise. Less expensive turbines are one way communities will be able to more easily take advantage of wind energy.

One successful example of a community wind installation is the Fox Islands Wind Project in Maine. The town's three turbines provide 30 percent of the community's electricity needs.[8] In Alaska, where fuel costs are more than three times the national average, a utility cooperative has integrated wind-generated electricity into its grids, successfully lowering costs in some remote villages. In one year, their wind turbines produced the same power as 99,191 gallons (375,479 L) of diesel fuel for a savings of $453,000.[9]

Community wind can be beneficial, but there are many implications for owners to consider.

While the initial investment in permits, turbines, and related equipment is expensive—offset somewhat by tax credits and other financial incentives—community wind has many benefits. Future energy profits stay in the community, projects generate jobs, and residents are assured of a clean—and usually cheaper—source of energy.

CHAPTER 10

HIGH WIND:
WINDMILLS IN THE SKY

It seems fitting that one of the most innovative areas of wind technology is in the air itself. If you have ever flown a kite, you know how strongly the wind can pull at the string. And while it may take a little effort to get the kite off the ground, once in the sky, it can stay up seemingly forever. You will probably reel it in before it comes down on its own. Now, picture a device flying high in the sky like a kite, but tethered to the ground and generating electricity. You have just imagined the cutting edge of wind energy: the flying wind turbine, formally known as airborne wind energy (AWE).

The reason kites can stay aloft so long, and with such force, is because wind speed increases with elevation. Winds at 30,000 feet (9,000 m) carry 20 times more energy than winds at sea level.[1] High-altitude winds are also more consistent, which means

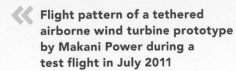

Flight pattern of a tethered airborne wind turbine prototype by Makani Power during a test flight in July 2011

wind power can be generated virtually 24 hours a day. AWE systems are being designed to take advantage of the massive energy potential contained in high-altitude winds.

A FLEDGLING INDUSTRY

In 2011, an international renewable energy consultant identified 22 companies with airborne wind projects at different stages of development.[2] The experimental flying airfoils, which are shaped like wings, boxes, kites, balloons, and gliders, may look quirky, but their inventors and investors are taking them very seriously.

All airborne wind turbines have a few things in common. They typically hover at approximately 1,300 feet (400 m), which means they would just skim the top of the 1,200-foot (370-m) Empire State Building. They are tethered to the ground, and they convert energy from the motion of the wind into electricity. The way these airborne turbines capture wind, however, varies as much as each one's unique design.

PROPELLER POWER

Corwin Hardham, a mechanical engineer with a PhD from Stanford University, got his idea for a flying wind turbine from kite surfing. He and the employees of his California-based company, Makani Power, have created a self-piloting, fixed-wing glider. It uses an onboard computer to

A Makani Power airborne wind turbine prototype is set up for a test flight in Alameda, California, on December 12, 2011.

steer it in large circles 1,000 feet (300 m) in the sky. Six small rotors at the front of the glider get it airborne like a helicopter. Then, the rotors turn forward. The wind spins them at up to 250 miles per hour (400 km/h), creating electricity that flows down the glider's high-voltage tether. Makani Power successfully flew their 20-kilowatt Wing 7 prototype with its 26-foot (8 m) wingspan in 2011. The company caught the interest of private and public investors. The cofounders of Internet giant Google invested $20 million in Hardham's company, and the US Department of Energy has invested $3 million. As of 2011, Makani Power expected to have a full-scale prototype completed in 2013, with commercial production to begin in 2015.[3]

In a grassy field near Santa Cruz, California, engineers and technicians intently monitor equipment and laptop computers. They are interrupted when a high-pitched whine draws their attention skyward. A rectangular box swoops noisily overhead, powered by fast-spinning rotor blades. It looks like a motorized kite, but this is no toy. It's a prototype on the cutting edge of wind energy—an airborne wind turbine.

This turbine's inventor, JoeBen Bevirt, came up with the idea during a bumpy airplane ride. "I realized that we had 200-mile-an-hour [320 km/h] tailwinds," he told *Discover* magazine. "So I started doing calculations on exactly how much power was in 200-mile-an-hour winds. By the time I landed, I was all fired up."[5]

Using wind to create energy is cheap, clean, and renewable, but it only works when the wind blows. Wind can drop off suddenly, which makes it difficult to rely on for consistent energy. The wind blows significantly stronger and steadier 1,000 to 2,000 feet (300 to 600 m) up, where Bevirt anticipates his turbines will one day fly.

Bevirt and his team at Joby Energy experimented with early designs for their airborne turbine, settling on a rectangular box shape. Fourteen rotors will lift the 200-foot (60 m) production model off the ground like a helicopter. A computer system will turn the self-piloting craft on its end and send it swooping in huge Ferris-wheel-like circles. Crosswinds will spin

JoeBen Bevirt and his
prototype airborne
wind turbine

the rotors at high speeds, and shafts connected to the rotors will feed directly into onboard generators. The turbine will be rated for two megawatts of electricity, about the same energy potential as many modern commercial turbines. However, because of the steadier and stronger winds at the higher altitude, annual output will be nearly twice that of a conventional turbine. Electricity will travel down a cable that will also keep the turbine tethered to the ground.

There are still many bugs to work out. Among Bevirt's biggest challenges are safely controlling the unmanned craft, quieting noisy rotors, and getting government approval. Is this edgy new technology worth the effort? Bevirt told *Discover*, "In order to have truly sustainable energy . . . we are going to need game-changing technology. I believe that technology is high-altitude wind."[6]

Another California company, Sky WindPower, is working on a design first developed by Australian engineering professor Bryan Roberts, one of the first people to work on harnessing high-altitude wind. Named one of the top 50 inventions of 2008 by *TIME* magazine, the company's flying generator is shaped like the letter *H*.[4] It relies on four large rotors, similar to those used in aircraft, to get it aloft. Once in the sky, wind spins the rotor blades to generate electricity and keep the craft airborne. The electric current is sent to the ground via its tether. The company flew a six-kilowatt prototype in 2007 and plans to complete a one-megawatt model by 2014.

REELING STRINGS

As the Ampyx PowerPlane glider lifts into the air like a kite, its tether unwinds from a ground-based winch. This unwinding motion spins a generator that creates electricity. When the tether reaches its end, the glider flies gently toward the ground station and the tether is reeled in. The process repeats as long as wind is available. Ampyx, a Dutch company, flew a ten-kilowatt PowerPlane prototype with an 18-foot (5.5 m) wingspan in 2010 and plans to have a one-megawatt model airborne in 2013.

Like the PowerPlane, a flexible airfoil by North Carolina company Windlift is tethered to a turning drum that creates electricity at a ground-based station. Windlift currently has a 12-kilowatt prototype and is working on a 20-kilowatt model. Windlift has received two development grants from the US Department of Defense.

WILL AWE TURBINES GET OFF THE GROUND?

With so many AWE systems in the works, it seems as though flying turbines will eventually become another wind-energy option. There are, however, technical bugs to work out and government regulations to consider before airborne wind turbines find a permanent place in the sky. The turbines must be able to take off, fly by themselves for days at a time in varying wind conditions, and land, all without a human pilot. Sophisticated control systems are crucial—no one wants a turbine the size of a semi truck falling on them. Another negative: electricity is lost through the long cable tethers, and some of the experimental turbines are noisy.

Airborne turbines may hinder airplanes and other air traffic, so they come under the

AWE AND THE FAA

At the end of 2011, the Federal Aviation Administration (FAA) published new rules regulating AWE test flights. Every test flight must get FAA approval and meet certain requirements. For each project, the developers must evaluate several things, including:

> impact of airborne turbines on radar
> visibility of turbines to aircraft
> safety of people in the air and on the ground
> consequences if a turbine tether breaks
> amount of airspace an AWE farm might require[7]

jurisdiction of the US government's Federal Aviation Administration (FAA). The FAA is currently considering its stance on AWE. Without government approval, airborne wind turbines will have to stay grounded. Investors are showing they are wary of sinking more money into this new technology. Developers have been hoping the FAA will create restricted flight zones above AWE farms so air traffic is not a problem.

OPPOSING AWE OPINIONS

As with any innovation that breaks new ground technologically, AWE garners both praise and criticism. Ken Caldeira, Stanford University climate scientist, stated, "If you tapped into one percent of the power in high-altitude winds, that would be enough to continuously power all civilization."[10] Fort Felker, a wind-power expert with NREL, counters this by pointing out, "The people doing airborne wind are visionaries, but none of them has brought a product to market that has the safety and reliability requirements of flight vehicles."[11]

Even with its drawbacks, AWE has much to offer. In addition to greater power due to increased wind speeds, airborne wind turbines promise a few advantages over conventional wind turbines. Airborne wind turbines don't require towers or long blades, so they use a fraction of the materials. This reduces weight, minimizes transportation issues, and cuts costs. Hardham of Makani Power expects the electricity from his turbine to cost only three cents per kilowatt.[8] That is approximately four cents cheaper than the per-kilowatt cost of wind power in 2010.[9] Even though some areas of the world have stronger high-altitude winds than others, high-altitude wind is everywhere. This means airborne wind turbines are not restricted to just a few ideal areas of land or sea. Another plus is that airborne wind turbines do not disrupt the landscape and are not as visible as commercial horizontal-axis turbines. In a few years, you may look up and see wind turbines flying over your head.

THE FUTURE OF WIND ENERGY

Researchers and designers are forging ahead with new wind innovations. As of 2011, financial support continues for wind developments, and new facilities continue to be built. According to the AWEA, as of 2011, wind power made up 35 percent of all new generating capacity added to the US grid since 2007— twice the capacity added by coal and nuclear power combined.[12] At the end of 2011, more than 8,400 megawatts of wind power capacity was under construction in the United States, topping 2010 installations for the same time period by 75 percent.[13] Multi-megawatt wind installations were planned for states across the country, including Kansas,

WIND LEADERS

In President Barack Obama's 2011 State of the Union address, he called for 80 percent of the nation's electricity to come from clean-energy sources by 2035. However, the United States lacked a cohesive renewable energy strategy as of 2011. This was not the case in other countries, including Denmark, Germany, and China. The Chinese government was pumping billions of dollars into renewable-energy technologies, including wind power. As Ron Pernick, a renewable-energy researcher and author, wrote in a 2011 article:

One of the . . . things that makes China and the [United States] so different is that Chinese national and regional leadership is now fully aligned behind clean tech[nology] as an economic development and jobs growth strategy. They aren't fighting amongst themselves about whether they should support clean energy, but are instead fighting to lead in the sector.[14]

"[There is] a long-term, consistent drop in clean energy technology costs, resulting from decades of hard work by tens of thousands of researchers, engineers, technicians, and people in operations and procurement. And it is not going to stop: in the next few years, the mainstream world is going to wake up to wind cheaper than gas, and rooftop solar power cheaper than daytime electricity. . . . We are clearly talking about a whole new game."[15]—**Justin Wu, analyst at Bloomberg New Energy Finance**

Pennsylvania, Wisconsin, Texas, Colorado, Illinois, Vermont, and Michigan.

Research is also being done on possibilities of wind-solar hybrid systems. When the wind isn't blowing, the sun may be out. A major advantage to any hybrid system is one system can cover inefficiencies created by the other half. In a wind-solar hybrid system, strong winter winds could be balanced by summer's sunny days. Batteries store electricity from both systems and provide backup power, typically for approximately one to three days. A generator is sometimes included as part of the system to charge the batteries when needed. Pairing solar cells with wind turbines may seem obvious, but wind-solar hybrid systems have only become popular in the past several years. Future research and innovations may create advances in these systems, or possibly even new sources for hybrid wind projects.

>> **Hybrid wind-solar turbines could take advantage of renewable energy in most weather.**

Wind power is steadily growing as a valuable addition to the world's energy supply, and it is one possible solution to our dependence on fossil fuels. The abundance of recent innovations in wind energy suggests wind may be the key to long-term sustainable energy use.

GLOSSARY

AERODYNAMIC—A shape that reduces drag from air movement.

GLOBAL WARMING—An increase in the overall temperature of the earth's atmosphere that is usually attributed to the greenhouse effect.

INTERMITTENT—Something that starts and stops or only occurs irregularly.

MANDATE—A formal order or command.

SUBSIDY—A grant of money, often from the government.

TAX INCENTIVE—A part of a tax code that encourages certain actions through reward of tax deductions or eliminations.

TURBINE—A machine that produces power when wind (or water or another gas) causes a wheel or rotor to revolve.

UTILITY—An organization that supplies resources such as electricity, gas, and water for the public in a given area.

UTILITY GRID—System that generates, transmits, and distributes electricity over a vast area.

VOLTAGE—The electric potential or difference in electric charge between two points in an electric circuit.

WIND FARM—A number of wind turbines used collectively to feed energy into an electric grid.

ADDITIONAL RESOURCES

SELECTED BIBLIOGRAPHY

Gipe, Paul. *Wind Power: Renewable Energy for Home, Farm, and Business.* White River Junction, VT: Chelsea Green, 2004. Print.

Righter, Robert W. *Wind Energy in America: A History.* Norman, OK: U of Oklahoma, 1996. Print.

Sathyajith, Mathew. *Wind Energy: Fundamentals, Resource Analysis, and Economics.* Berlin: Springer, 2006. Print.

FURTHER READINGS

Langwith, Jacqueline. *Renewable Energy.* Farmington Hills, MI: Greenhaven, 2008. Print.

Ollhoff, Jim. *Wind and Water.* Minneapolis, MN: ABDO, 2010. Print.

Spilsbury, Richard. *Wind Power.* New York: PowerKids, 2011. Print.

WEB LINKS

To learn more about wind energy, visit ABDO Publishing Company online at
www.abdopublishing.com. Web sites about wind energy are featured on our Book Links page.
These links are routinely monitored and updated to provide the most current information available.

FOR MORE INFORMATION

For more information on this subject, contact or visit the following organizations:

AMERICAN WIND ENERGY ASSOCIATION (AWEA)
1501 M Street, NW, Suite 1000, Washington, DC 20005
202-383-2500
http://www.awea.org

The AWEA is a national trade association of wind-industry manufacturers, suppliers, and researchers.
Contact the organization for more information on the wind industry.

ENERGY EFFICIENCY AND RENEWABLE ENERGY (EERE), US DEPARTMENT OF ENERGY
Office of the Assistant Secretary
Energy Efficiency and Renewable Energy
Mail Stop EE-1, Department of Energy, Washington, DC 20585
http://www.eere.energy.gov

The EERE is a US Department of Energy office dedicated to research and implementation of clean-energy technologies. Wind Program information can be found online at the organization's Web site.

SOURCE NOTES

CHAPTER 1. WIND ENERGY AT A GLANCE

1. "Fast Facts." *International Energy Agency.* OECD/IEA, n.d. Web. 8 Aug. 2012.

CHAPTER 2. THE HISTORY OF WIND ENERGY

1. "History." *Windmill Gallery.* Windmill Gallery, n.d. Web. 8 Aug. 2012.

2. "1973–1974 Oil Crisis." *Slaying the Dragon of Debt.* University of California, n.d. Web. 8 Aug. 2012.

3. "20% Wind Energy by 2030." *Nrel.gov.* US Department of Energy, EERE, July 2008. Web. 8 Aug. 2012.

4. Jan Null and Cristina Archer. "Wind Power: The Ultimate Renewable Energy Source." *Weatherwise.* Taylor & Francis Group, July/August 2008. Web. 8 Aug. 2012.

CHAPTER 3. ASSESSING THE WIND

1. John Farrell and David Morris. *Energy Self-Reliant States.* 2nd ed. Minneapolis: New Rules Project, 2010. Print. 10.

2. Paul Gipe. *Wind Power: Renewable Energy for Home, Farm, and Business.* White River Junction, VT: Chelsea Green, 2004. Print. 30–31.

CHAPTER 4. TURBINE TYPES

1. "What It Costs For A Residential Wind Turbine." *What It Costs.* What It Costs, n.d. Web. 8 Aug. 2012.

2. "FAQ–Output." *National Wind Watch.* National Wind Watch, n.d. Web. 8 Aug. 2012.

3. "Products–Glossary." *Prudent Energy VRB Systems.* Prudent Energy Corporation, n.d. Web. 8 Aug. 2012.

4. Ryan Wiser and M. Bolinger. "2010 Wind Technologies Market Report." *EERE.* US Department of Energy, June 2011. Web. 27 May 2012.

CHAPTER 5. BENEFITS OF WIND ENERGY

1. Mathew Sathyajith. *Wind Energy: Fundamentals, Resource Analysis, and Economics.* Berlin: Springer, 2006. 179. *Google Book Search.* Web. 27 May 2012.

2. Ramit Plushnick-Masti. "Texas Drought 2011: Power Projects Endangered." *HuffPost Green.* Huffington Post, n.d. Web. 8 Aug. 2012.

3. Kevin D. Williamson. "Disinherit the Wind." *National Review* 20 June 2011: 44. *EBSCO.* Web. 22 May 2012.

4. Jan M. Olsen. "EU Agency: Air Pollution Costs Exceed $134 Billion." *Phys.Org.* Phys.Org, 24 Nov. 2011. Web. 8 Aug. 2012.

5. Stephen Lacey. "Wind Electricity To Be Fully Competitive With Natural Gas by 2016, Says Bloomberg New Energy Finance." *Renewable Energy World.* Renewable Energy World, 15 Nov. 2011. Web. 27 May 2012.

6. Ken Zweibel. "Should Solar Photovoltaics be Deployed Sooner Because of Long Operating Life at Low Predictable Cost?" *Energy Policy.* Elsevier, 5 Mar. 2010. Web. 27 May 2012.

7. Stephen Lacey. "Wind Electricity To Be Fully Competitive With Natural Gas by 2016, Says Bloomberg New Energy Finance." *Renewable Energy World.* Renewable Energy World, 15 Nov. 2011. Web. 27 May 2012.

8. "Energy." *PollingReport.com.* Polling Report, 2012. Web. 27 May 2012.

9. Lydia Saad. "In U.S., Expanding Energy Output Still Trumps Green Concerns." *Gallup.com.* Gallup, 16 Mar. 2011. Web. 27 May 2012.

10. "American Wind Power (Brochure)." *American Wind Energy Association.* American Wind Energy Association, n.d. Web. 8 Aug. 2012.

CHAPTER 6. DRAWBACKS OF WIND ENERGY

1. Matthew L. Wald. "Wind Power Unreliable? Build More Turbines." *New York Times*. New York Times, 20 Jan. 2010. Web. 8 Aug. 2012.

2. Tom Zeller Jr. "For Those Near, the Miserable Hum of Clean Energy." *New York Times*. New York Times, 5 Oct. 2010. Web. 29 May 2012.

3. Ibid.

4. Gregg Vanderheiden. "About Decibels." *Trace R&D Center, University of Wisconsin–Madison*. University of Wisconsin, 19 Mar. 2010. Web. 8 Aug 2012.

5. John Anderson. "Utility Scale Wind Energy and Sound." *American Wind Energy Association*. American Wind Energy Association, n.d. Web. 8 Aug. 2012.

6. National Wind Coordinating Committee. "Avian Collisions with Wind Turbines." *National Wind Coordinating Collaborative*. National Wind Coordinating Collaborative, Aug. 2001. Web. 8 Aug. 2012.

7. Ibid.

8. "Bat Fatalities at Wind Turbines: Investigating the Causes and Consequences." *USGS*. US Geological Survey, 8 Aug. 2012. Web. 8 Aug. 2012.

9. Umair Irfan. "Bats and Birds Face Serious Threats From Growth of Wind Energy." *New York Times*. New York Times, 8 Aug. 2011. Web. 8 Aug. 2012.

10. Ibid.

11. Jenny Jones. "New Wind Turbine Blades Bigger, Lighter, Stronger." *Civil Engineering* Oct. 2011: 38. *Academic Search Elite*. Web. 29 May 2012.

12. "Tougher, Lighter Wind Turbine Blade Developed: Polyurethane Reinforced with Carbon Nanotubes." *ScienceDaily*. Science Daily, 30 Aug 2011. Web. 8 Aug. 2012.

13. Robert W. Righter. *Wind Energy in America: A History*. Norman, OK: U of Oklahoma, 1996. 31. *Google Books Search*. Web. 29 May 2012.

14. Kathleen Zip. "Bigger Turbines Come with Bigger Transport Headaches." *Windpower Engineering and Development*. WTWH Media, 1 Oct. 2010. Web. 8 Aug. 2012.

15. Ryan Wiser and M. Bolinger. "2010 Wind Technologies Market Report." *EERE*. US Department of Energy, June 2011. Web. 27 May 2012.

CHAPTER 7. ONSHORE WIND: WIND FARMS

1. "Wind Energy Myths." *Canwea*. Canadian Wind Energy Association, 2008. Web. 8 Aug. 2012.

2. "Wind Turbines on Farmland May Benefit Crops." *US News Science*. US News & World Report LP, 20 Dec. 2010. Web. 8 Aug. 2012.

3. Nino Marchetti. "How Far Apart Should Wind Turbines Be?" *EarthTechling*. EarthTechling, 29 Nov. 2010. Web. 8 Aug. 2012.

4. Chris Rose. "World's Largest Wind Farm in Wyoming to Be Equipped with 1,000 Wind Turbines." *Governors Wind Energy Coalition*. Governors Wind Energy Coalition, 20 Jan. 2012. Web. 8 Aug. 2012.

5. Catherine Clabby. "A Fish of an Idea." *American Scientist* Sept.–Oct. 2011: 382. *Academic Search Elite*. Web. 29 May 2012.

6. Tiffany Hsu. "Wind Turbines Growing Taller and More Powerful." *Los Angeles Times*. Los Angeles Times, 24 July 2011. Web. 8 Aug. 2012.

7. "Operational and Maintenance Costs for Wind Turbines." *Wind Measurement International*. Wind Measurement International, n.d. Web. 8 Aug. 2012.

8. Tiffany Hsu. "Wind Turbines Growing Taller and More Powerful." *Los Angeles Times*. Los Angeles Times, 24 July 2011. Web. 8 Aug. 2012.

9. David Ferris. "Innovate: New Designs in Wind Power." *Sierra* May–June 2010: 27. *Academic Search Elite*. Web. 29 May 2012.

10. "Production Tax Credit for Renewable Energy." *Union of Concerned Scientists*. Union of Concerned Scientists, 13 Sept. 2011. Web. 8 Aug. 2012.

11. T. Boone Pickens. "Get With the Plan." *National Review Online*. National Review Online, 20 June 2011. Web. 7 Sept. 2012.

CHAPTER 8. BIG WIND: WIND FARMS AT SEA

1. Alan Brown. "Study Proposes Goal-Driven Regulations for Offshore Wind." *Mechanical Engineering* 133.8 (2011): 12. *Academic Search Elite*. Web. 29 May 2012.

2. "Cape Wind Gets Permit For Offshore Wind Farm Clean Water Act Compliance." *HuffPost Green*. Huffington Post, 6 Jan. 2011. Web. 8 Aug. 2012.

3. "Project at a Glance." *Cape Wind*. Cape Wind, n.d. Web. 8 Aug. 2012.

4. Dominique Roddier and Joshua Weinstein. "Floating Wind Turbines." *Mechanical Engineering* (2010): 28–32. *Academic Search Elite*. Web. 30 May 2012.

5. "Offshore Wind Energy." *Ocean Energy Council*. Ocean Energy Council, 2012. Web. 8 Aug. 2012.

6. "Windmills on the Mind." *Professional Engineering*. Professional Engineering, 5 July 2011. Web. 8 Aug. 2012.

7. "Offshore Wind Energy." *Ocean Energy Council*. Ocean Energy Council, 2012. Web. 8 Aug. 2012.

8. Matthew L. Wald. "Washington Invests in Making Wind Pay." *New York Times*. New York Times, 7 Feb. 2011. Web. 8 Aug. 2012.

9. Dominique Roddier and Joshua Weinstein. "Floating Wind Turbines." *Mechanical Engineering* (2010): 28–32. *Academic Search Elite*. Web. 30 May 2012.

10. Rena Marie Pacella. "The Next-Gen Wind Turbine." *Popular Science* Apr. 2010: 42–43. *Academic Search Elite*. Web. 30 May 2012.

CHAPTER 9. SMALL WIND: HOMES, BUSINESSES, AND COMMUNITIES

1. "2010 U.S. Small Wind Turbine Market Report." *American Wind Energy Association*. American Wind Energy Association, n.d. Web. 8 Aug. 2012.

2. Ryan Wiser and M. Bolinger. "2010 Wind Technologies Market Report." *EERE*. US Department of Energy, June 2011. Web. 27 May 2012.

3. Greg Pahl. "Community Supported Wind Power." *Mother Earth News* June–July 2008: 44–48. *Academic Search Complete*. Web. 30 May 2012.

4. Sarah Parsons. "Rooftop Wind Farm." *Popular Science* Oct. 2011: 20. *Academic Search Elite*. Web. 30 May 2012.

5. "Up on the Rooftop." *Industry Week/IW* Sept. 2009: 53. *Academic Search Elite*. Web. 30 May 2012.

6. Kari Lydersen. "Green Living: Wind Turbines Power a Bronx Apartment Complex." *Christian Science Monitor*. Christian Science Monitor, 7 Aug. 2010. Web. 8 Aug. 2012.

7. Libby Tucker. "Old Turbines Get a Second Wind Through Remanufacturing." *New York Times*. New York Times, 26 Jan. 2009. Web. 8 Aug. 2012.

8. Alan Borst. "Community Wind: Maine Island Community Lowering Energy Costs with Wind-Power Project." *USDA Rural Development*. United States Department of Agriculture, n.d. Web. 8 Aug. 2012.

9. Anne Todd. "Wind Power: Key to Reducing Costs for Isolated Alaska Villages." *Rural Cooperatives* 1 May 2009: 28–29. Print. *EBSCO*. Web. 30 May 2012.

10. Paul Gipe. *Wind Power: Renewable Energy for Home, Farm, and Business*. White River Junction, VT: Chelsea Green, 2004. Print. 13.

CHAPTER 10. HIGH WIND: WINDMILLS IN THE SKY

1. Christine Blackman. "High-Altitude Winds: The Greatest Source of Concentrated Energy on Earth." *Stanford University News*. Stanford University, 23 June 2009. Web. 8 Aug. 2012.

2. "Market Report High Altitude Wind Energy." *GL Garrad Hassan*. GL Group, Aug. 2011. Web. 8 Aug. 2012.

3. Energy NOW. "The Makani Airborne Wind Turbine (Video)." *Vimeo*. Vimeo, n.d. Web. 8 Aug. 2012.

4. Jim Kozubek. "Airborne Wind Energy Industry Struggles To Fly." *Idealab*. TPM Idea Lab, 4 Nov. 2011. Web. 30 May 2012.

5. Erik Vance. "Inherit the Wind." *Discover* Dec. 2010. *Academic Search Elite*. Web. 30 May 2012.

6. Ibid.

7. "Notification for Airborne Wind Energy Systems (AWES)." *Federal Register*. National Archives and Records Administration, n.d. Web. 8 Aug. 2012.

8. Energy NOW. "The Makani Airborne Wind Turbine (Video)." *Vimeo*. Vimeo, n.d. Web. 8 Aug. 2012.

9. "Renewable Energy for America." *Natural Resources Defense Council*. Natural Resources Defense Council, n.d. Web. 8 Aug. 2012.

10. Christine Blackman. "High-Altitude Winds: The Greatest Source of Concentrated Energy on Earth." *Stanford University News*. Stanford University, 23 June 2009. Web. 8 Aug. 2012.

11. James Vlahos. "Up in the Air: How Flying Turbines Will Change Wind Power." *Popular Mechanics*. Hearst Communication, 30 Mar. 2011. Web. 8 Aug. 2012.

12. Lindsay Morris. "Wind Energy Outlook 2012: An Uncertain Forecast." *RenewableEnergyWorld.com*. RenewableEnergyWorld.com, 8 Dec. 2011. Web. 8 Aug. 2012.

13. Ibid.

14. Ron Pernick. "The Future of Clean Tech and Why I Can't Stop Thinking About China." *Renewablenergyworld.com*. RenewableEnergyWorld.com, 11 Nov. 2011. Web. 8 Aug. 2012.

15. "Onshore Wind Energy to Reach Parity with Fossil Fuel Electricity by 2016." *Bloomberg New Energy Finance*. Bloomberg L.P., 10 Nov. 2011. Web. 8 Aug. 2012.

INDEX

ABOUT THE AUTHOR

Melissa Higgins is the author of numerous nonfiction books for children and young adults, with topics ranging from science and technology to social studies and mental health. She also writes short stories and novels. Before pursuing a writing career, Higgins worked as a counselor in schools and private practice.

ABOUT THE CONTENT CONSULTANT

Erik Nordman received his PhD from the SUNY College of Environmental Science and Forestry in Syracuse, New York. He is currently an associate professor of natural resources management at Grand Valley State University in Allendale, Michigan. His teaching focus is on natural resource economics and policy, geographic information systems, and renewable energy. Dr. Nordman was awarded a Fulbright Scholar grant to teach and study wind energy at Kenyatta University in Nairobi, Kenya. Dr. Nordman is also the principal investigator for the West Michigan Wind Assessment project. The project assesses the possible implementation of wind turbines on the coast of West Michigan, taking economic, environmental, and social aspects into consideration.